IT'S KINDA PERSONAL.

Raw emotion. Unfiltered pain.

Samantha Dee

For people hurting and suffering, in silence or not.

For people who have hurt me.

For people I have hurt.

For you. You know who you are.

"People are people and have their own insecurities. We cannot make anyone do, feel, change, or say anything. We are only responsible for our own actions, words, thoughts, etc. You do not have to take on the world. Keep being kind, caring, and giving, and you are on the correct path ... I love you, let it go."

-My beautiful mother.

MURDER BY MIND.

My mind
It's like a room
Only it has no door
No exit
No way out
And the walls
They're closing in
Taunting me
Crushing my bones
It's like a room
Only it's not
My mind
It's killing me

WHEN IT ENDED.

You went looking for answers at the bottom of
bottles
You wanted the taste of me out of your mouth
Somewhere it lived for some time
Until you drowned me out

I went back to smoking packs of cigarettes a day
I wanted to light fire to my insides
Somewhere you explored often
Until I burnt you out

We drowned in the vodka you drank
We burned with the cigarettes I lit
As if our love hadn't killed us enough
As if we hadn't already destroyed each other

FIRE IN THE HEART OF HER HOME.

She's building a home in your arms that used to be
mine
I wonder if she knows as soon as she moves in
You're gonna burn her house to the ground

BLINDFOLDED BY YOU.

I see your blue eyes in the sky
When I wake up
It hurts so bad
I've stopped looking outside
You see my brown eyes in your coffee
That you drink scorching
To burn my name
Out of your mouth

DON'T GO, BUT LEAVE.

So I screamed
I screamed for him to leave me
Once between my sobs and gasps for air and then
at the top of my lungs
I screamed it once more as tears started flowing
out of his eyes and I saw them glistening under
the street lights, but I didn't care
I screamed it again and again
I think somewhere between the sixth and seventh
time he finally realized how bad he wanted to stay
I think somewhere between the sixth and seventh
time I finally convinced myself I wanted him to
leave

STORMS ARE FUCKING CATASTROPHIC.

For fucks sake it's 12 AM
I'm wondering
Why do I have a mind full of storms?
And why does Thunder beat louder than my heart
And why does Lightning strike my insides so hard
And why does Rain heavily flood my eyes

For fucks sake it's 1 AM
I'm wondering
Do you think storms are beautiful or catastrophic?
Are you a storm chaser or are you afraid Of the
thunder that could rip you apart
Or are you afraid Of the lightning that could shock
your heart
Or are you afraid Of the rain that could drown out
your pain

For fucks sake it's the hours of the AM
I'm wondering
Why do I have a mind full of storms?
Do you think storms are beautiful?

I LOVE YOU IN THE PARALLEL UNIVERSE
JUST AS MUCH AS I DO IN THIS ONE AND
MAYBE THAT'S WHY I STILL MAKE
EXCUSES FOR OUR FAILURE.

In a parallel universe we belong together
That has to be it
That has to be why every single kiss felt right
Why we loved each other so goddamn much
We belong together
Just not in this universe
We can't be together here
That has to be it
That has to be why every kiss turned into stabs at
my heart
Why every goddamn "love you" began to burn
your throat
We don't belong together
Not in this universe
We can be together there
That has to be it
In a parallel universe we belong together

MOM...DAD...

I'm so sorry.
I know you're blaming yourself, but please don't.
You did everything right... everything you could. It
couldn't have been your fault.
The loneliness that lingered inside of me finally
took over and turned everything black.
I will spend the rest of what would have been my
life missing you.

Know this mom, dad... I am with you. Forever.
Always.
I'm the thunder that shakes the house and wakes
you up when you're lying in bed half asleep.
I'm the beautiful rays of sunshine that sneak
through the clouds on a gloomy day.
I'm the rainbow that shines so bright after a nasty
rain storm.
I am everything that is so beautifully destructive.
Because that is all that I was on Earth.
Destructive. Beautiful.

MY YOUNGEST BROTHER...

I'm so sorry.
I hope you feel it in your heart how much I loved you. Carry it with you.
Remember our laughs when you think of me.
Remember our silly car rides with music blasting.
Please remember to laugh at our memories.
Please remember to keep blasting our favorite song.

And know this, little one.... I am with you.
When you're reminiscing on your big sis and smiling, laughing, crying, screaming. I'm doing it right there alongside of you. I promise.
When you're blaring music in the car and singing so loud you can't hear the music. So am I. In the front seat looking at how handsome you turned out to be.
I'm with you. Forever. Always.

MY YOUNGER BROTHER...

I'm so sorry.
You were my best friend. You are and forever will be to me.
Thank you for always checking in on me. Thank you for loving me. Thank you.
You have experienced so much loss. Death. Pain. I am so fucking sorry. I am.
You are strong. You are beautiful. You are the world.

Know this, little brother…. I am here.
When you need me. I am here.
When you don't know who else to go to because it was always me. I am here.
Look at the sky on a clear summer night and I'll show you.
Sit in my bedroom when you need me and I will be there. I promise.
I am here. Forever. Always.

MY OLDER BROTHER...

I'm so sorry.
You were my role model. It just seemed too impossible to me.
Your success is superb, and I was so proud of the person you have become. I always will be.
You were my comic relief in life.
We joked about everything. We laughed about anything. We had so much fun.
Remember me for that.
Remember my twisted sense of humor and the way it brought yours out too.

Know this, big brother.... I'll be there.
Listen for me when you think of a dark joke in your head but can't say it out loud to anyone.
Say it for me. Please.
Laugh your ass off in your car. Alone. To your own joke.
Do that for me. Please.
Believe it or not I am not gone. I will be there.
Laughing. Crying. Joking.
I'll be there. Forever. Always.

YOU…

I'm so sorry.
We worked on this for days. Weeks. Months.
I told you I was improving. I didn't want to worry
you.
Do not remember me for my sadness.
Remember me for our love.
Remember our hugs. Kisses. Cuddles. Smiles.
Laughs. Dances. Adventures. Talks.
Please remember the good times we had.
Please remember me.

Know this, I died loving you.
I guess that means I will always love you.
When your heart is broken. Remember.
When you move on and compare her to me.
Remember I love you. But I cannot be there.
Let her. Let her be there. Let her love you.
I love you. Forever. Always.

HER...

I'm so sorry.
I'm so sorry for hurting him.
But.
If you are reading this, he knows it's you.
If you are reading this, he loves you.

Know this, I love you too.
Forever. Always.

ONE SIDED TYPE OF LOVE.

Maybe if you knew how painful it is to love you
while you love her, you'd come back
Maybe then you'd look at me with those deep
brown eyes I'm reminded of by my cup of coffee
every morning and you'd see in me what you see
in her
If you knew how painful it is to see you hold her

If you knew how painful it is
Maybe then you'd come back
Maybe then

TURN IT OFF, TURN IT OFF, TURN IT OFF.

What are you thinking? My mind is racing like running a marathon, only out of shape and hardly keeping up. I can't seem to grasp him, or even the idea of him, let alone his mind. *Let me in.* I wish I could turn these thoughts off. Just flip a switch and BAM! they're gone. What would it be like? You know, not to have voices in my head all speaking at the same time, filling my ears with buzzing of bees that seem so real but they're just in my head. Nobody else can hear these goddamn things. Is it bad to say that I'm glad they're endangered? Maybe they'll get the fuck out of my head and go somewhere that's important. My body shifts as he moves his arm from under me. I feel his chest rise as he inhales the sweet, sweet air that we share, and fall again as he lets it back out. How blessed am I to share this air with someone so impeccable? *I want to be your oxygen. Breathe me in, utilize me as a lifeline, let me experience the artwork of your intertwined veins running through that body I crave so much.* I'd flip the switch right now. I swear I would.

NOT ME AND THE OCEAN.

I remember looking into his eyes so deeply and
thinking the blue was going to spill out and take
me into his ocean with waves so powerful they
captivated anything they came across without a
care in the world of what it might be.
He was the ocean- beautiful, daring and limitless -
immune to the pain he caused.
I remember the first time he looked at me and the
rush of water that came with it, catching me
completely off guard and knocking me over only
to be caught by another wave coming from the
opposite direction, leading me to my feet again.
He convinced me I could lean on him because he
would always be there to catch me with his
reliable tides.
I remember our first conversation and how both
the sun and his words made me feel warm inside
while the sound of his voice and his waves created
a melody I could've listened to all day.
He made me feel like the world, even though he
was the world with an area taking up more surface
than I would ever experience in my lifetime.

I remember the love I felt for him and how very intense it was, growing larger and larger as his sea level rose, exposing me to new parts of him I couldn't wait to explore.

He led me into his abyss and told me not to worry or look back, that he would take care of me with his gentle touch.

I remember the subtle way his low tides turned to high tides and intensified his every move, causing more hurt than happy and destroying me a little more with every waking breath I took.

He never fought the moon and its darkness, he just let it pull and effect his body of water, which only pulled me deeper and deeper into his trenches.

I remember the first fight and the way his words cut so deep into my skin while he continued to crash his waves into me, knocking me over and not leading me to my feet with his reliable tides, but instead leaving me at the bottom of his ocean. He let his salt water burn in the wounds he created in my skin.

I remember praying for the surface of his water while I laid at the bottom feeling hopeless and empty, fearful of opening my mouth to scream because his waters would pour inside of me and make my lungs panic.

He would win if I let that happen. I couldn't let him win.

I remember our last conversation and the way his tides pulled me in and trapped me in his current which was nearly impossible to escape from.

He finally let me go, but he would always take up 60% of my body.

I remember being young and being afraid of the ocean but never understanding why... Until I met him.

He was the ocean.

SEEING YOU IN MY COFFEE PROBABLY MEANS I'M CRAZY.

I swear my coffee used to be just coffee
And then I met you
Now my coffee can never just be coffee again

The first sip makes my lips feel warm like yours did
when you kissed me in the morning after cuddling
all night long

All I want is my coffee to just be
simple.fucking.coffee

EMPTY. BUT FULL OF YOU.

"Describe to me exactly how you feel"
"Just spill it all"
All I could say was empty
All I could feel was emptiness
Not anger
Not sadness
Not spite
Not jealousy
Just fucking emptiness

QUESTION FROM MY ELEVEN-YEAR-OLD BROTHER.

"Tell me exactly what it feels like to have your heart broken?"
I wanted to tell him all the little details, like how bad it hurt to breathe. How thinking about every breath I had to take without him slowly ruined me because every breath I took was supposed to be with him, how it was a blood gushing gash to the aorta that left all my insides spilling out, that it was a long hard sob into my already tear soaked pillow, ripping my chest wide open at the thought of being lost, it was everything I thought would hold together deteriorating right in front of my eyes, how desperately I craved the nightmares I had while I was asleep, because even those were better than being awake, that no one understood me and I felt so alone and every night I found myself in an empty parking lot crying because it was the only place that didn't feel like him. But I didn't.
Instead I just said, "You don't wanna know."

CRYING IS FOR THE BROKEN HEARTED.

He broke my heart and now my best friends are 3
AM and my bathroom floor that holds me tighter
than he ever did

WHAT YOU DON'T KNOW WON'T MAKE YOU LOVE ME AGAIN.

You don't know this
But that one Sunday that you were half asleep on
my chest
While I rubbed your head because something
inside it wanted to cause you pain
You blurted out "I love you" for the first time
And I whispered it back into your sleepy ears
You don't know this
But I love you to hell and back
And I always will

I WAS ON THE SIDE OF THE ROAD WITH A FLAT TIRE...

I hit a pot hole and all of a sudden I heard a pop
and felt my car drive like I was on a road of
marbles
Fuck
I pulled over and got out of my piece of junk, hand
me down, 2009 Ford Focus, and sure enough I had
a flat
What a perfect representation of my life
I had a flat tire on the side of the road while other
people went by on their way to places I'd surely
never go
The tire was me and the cars were everyone else
and I was always on the side by myself
What a perfect representation of my life

REPEAT AFTER ME.

It doesn't matter if you love him anymore because
He doesn't love you
He doesn't love you so you need to Love yourself
Love yourself enough to Pick yourself up
Pick yourself up off your bathroom floor when it's
3 am and all you feel is Pain
Pain will haunt you in ways you never knew
possible but you have to Fight it
Fight it like you fight your friends who say he's not
worth it until they Stop
Stop fighting your friends who say you deserve
better and Believe it
Believe it when he acts like he doesn't care
because I promise you He doesn't
He doesn't care when it's 3 AM and you're on the
floor by the toilet because the pain has spread to
every organ in your body and he doesn't care
when it's 1 PM and you still feel like your world
just ended but It didn't
It didn't end just because you two did and he is
not the world no matter how many times you
swore he was because You are
You are the whole world and every beautiful thing
it contains so Love yourself

Love yourself like you loved him and don't stop there because this time you're loving someone who actually deserves it

KEEP ON KEEPING ON BECAUSE ONE DAY YOU WON'T HAVE TO CONVINCE YOURSELF YOU'RE OKAY ANYMORE.

Keep faith
Even if it means you're on your knees in a gravel parking lot screaming to a God you struggle to believe in anymore, even if it means your knees are bloody and cut down to the bone

Keep holding on
Even if it means you're hanging from a bridge with a body of water underneath you and letting go seems so much easier, even if it means your hands are full of blisters and sweaty enough to slip at any second

Keep breathing
Even if it means every exhale is a relief like the knife is being pulled out and every inhale comes with bracing yourself for the next stab, even if it means your lungs are weak and you don't know how much more you can take

Keep thinking

Even if it means feelings pain so diminishing that
you feel as if you're less than you are every second
you let the thoughts take over, even if it means
your head hurts and your demons haunt you every
time you're alone

Keep hurting
Even if it means emotional pain turns physical and
everything hurts, even if it means staying in bed
for days because you feel too weak to move

Keep loving
Even if it means getting hurt repeatedly and
thinking you aren't enough, even if it means your
heart is in your hands because somebody ripped it
out and left

IF A PERSON CRIES WHEN NO ONE IS AROUND DO THEY MAKE A SOUND?

Your eyes are full of pain
Just because you only let it out behind closed
doors doesn't mean it doesn't hurt all the time

ARE YOU CHANTING 'FORGET ME NOT'?

I'm going to forget you
One day I'll wake up and I won't taste your name
in my mouth or feel striking pain in my throat as I
say it repeatedly desperately trying to make it
sound like less of a word
I'm going to forget your name
One day I'll listen to your favorite song and I won't
hear you singing it at the top of your lungs as I
drive the back roads with the windows down the
way we used to
I'm going to forget your voice
One day I'll wake up without hearing "I love you"
playing repeatedly in the sound of your voice in
my ears
I'm going to forget you

OBSESSIVE COMPULSIVE DISORDER.

I shut the door ten times when I got home from walking the block four times because something didn't feel right. Did it lock? Did it lock? Did it? Did it lock? Is the door locked? Is it locked? Did it lock? Did it, did it lock, did it? I went to the store to buy one thing and couldn't leave until I straightened out all the candy bars that made me shake because of the pile they were in. They didn't belong there. They needed to be where they belonged. Put them where they belong. Put them away. I stood in line and rubbed my finger against my palm in circles and waited until it was my turn.

The girl in front of me had a tag sticking out and her friend fixed it and said, "I'm so OCD."

TELL ME, DOES IT?

Doesn't it hurt to see the person you loved
begging on their knees for you?
*Doesn't it hurt to be begging on your knees for a
person who no longer loves you?*
Did you find happiness in ruining theirs?
Did you lose happiness trying to be theirs?
Does your heart even flinch at the way their eyes
are swollen and red from crying all night while you
were sleeping soundly?
*Does your heart heal at the fact that they can
sleep at night knowing you're in immense pain?*

I DIDN'T MEAN TO.

I didn't mean to ruin my brother's birthday dinner by sitting in the car crying because I was incapable of being in a chair at our favorite restaurant with circle tables embellished with blue tiles that reminded me of the color of your eyes, It Just Happened

It Just Happened to be our waitress, the one we requested every time we went out who asked me if I'd be having our usual. I told her our usual burned to Hell and that I wouldn't be ordering anything because the thought of us apart made me feel Sick To My Stomach

Sick To My Stomach I felt as I ran out of the restaurant wiping my tears with the back of my hand attempting to expunge the pain from my face to hide my weakness from The World

The World seemed so dull without you, something I swore I'd never live to know because you held my hands and looked me in the eyes and said "I Love You"

"I Love You" I screamed in the car over and over again hoping that in some universe the car was your mind and all you could hear was me screaming "I love you" repeatedly, forcing you to Come Back

"Come Back" I yelled next, into my hands this time so in that other universe you wouldn't be able to hear it, I didn't want you to see my weakness, I didn't want you to know how desperately I Needed You

I Needed You and I only told you once and it didn't seem to matter to you, I should have known the severity of the situation when I never once heard you say that you needed me or that you couldn't possibly live without me, but I didn't realize until It Was Too Late

It Was Too Late to walk back into the restaurant because I had already ruined it, but I didn't want to sit in the car anymore, so I got out and shut the door behind me and flinched at the sound of the slam because it was all Too Familiar

Too Familiar was the sound of a slamming door, after arguing that was your thing, but you always opened it back up, said sorry and took me into Your Arms

Your Arms were a safe place where I went when my house didn't feel like home and in those moments, you were home, you were supposed to continue to be Home

Home is where I wanted to go but instead, I took off running, first through the parking lot and then down the concrete roads of the entire plaza running as fast as my legs would allow, trying to run you Out Of My Mind

Out Of My Mind you didn't want to go, haunting my thoughts was a new hobby of yours, I started running faster and faster hoping my mind would finally escape the thought of you and be free, but I was running in circles and Nothing Seemed To Work

Nothing Seemed To Work out for me after I let you slip out of my life, ruining my brothers birthday dinner and many other things after that because I wasn't able to Get You Out Of My Mind

Get You Out Of My Mind was an alarm I started setting on my phone for 8 am every day, which seemed like a good idea, but I knew that no matter how hard I tried you'd always be on my mind and I Would Never Be Able To Forget You

I Would Never Be Able To Forget You and that
might be what hurt the most, I knew you'd never
fully escape my mind, and I knew that you'd never
think of me the way I thought of you, but one day
you'd see me with someone else and ask yourself,
"Why Did I Let Go?"
"Why Did I Let Go?" I asked myself until the 5
words didn't sound like words anymore, I was
afraid that if I gave up you would Come Back
Come Back is something I Don't Scream Anymore
I Don't Scream Anymore

I STILL THINK ABOUT YOU.

How does it feel? I wonder.
Tell me, please? I beg.
I stare at your headstone with you right under.
6 feet. Approximately how close I am to death.
6 feet too fucking many.
Living without you is unbearable.
The sun doesn't shine as bright anymore. The
clouds are always in front of it.
All I see is the rays that everyone says symbolize
you.
They're not you so I don't want them.
The flowers are dead, and the leaves are dying
too.
When you left everything left with you.

I PROMISE TO LOVE YOU.

When it's 2 am and you can't sleep because
there's a sadness inside of you that's slowly eating
you away.
I'll hold you, no matter how tired I am.
I'll rub your head the way you like and tell you that
it's all going to be okay.
I'll listen to your tears and wipe them away until
you have none left to shed.

A COMPLICATED IRREGULAR NETWORK OF PASSAGES IN WHICH IT IS DIFFICULT TO FIND ONE'S WAY.

You don't want to get lost in me.
A labyrinth.
Once you do there's no getting out.
There's no getting out, it's a trap. You'll dazzle in confusion between my thoughts of harm and my love for life, my mind goes back and forth between the two like a fucking seesaw.
You'll finally get weighed down by the harm and jump off the seesaw of confusion and right on to a mood swing that'll fly you through hundreds of emotions at once until your body can't possibly take anymore and you wonder how in the hell a mind could work this way so you jump off when you experience the fear and you land somewhere you wish you wouldn't have
A pit of emptiness surrounds you and before you can scream for help it caves in on your vulnerable body leaving you feeling emptier than humanly possible and you know that you're full of organs, tissue, bones and blood but god damn it you just feel like none of it is there until finally you reach
My fucking mind. The black hole.

MAGICIAN OF BETRAYAL AND HEARTBREAK.

The first time you said you loved me my heart was
beating so fast I thought it was going to beat out
of my chest and surrender to the sound of your
voice
You promised me it would be okay if it did
because you'd be gentle and keep it safe always
I reminded myself of your promise as I cut my
body open and let you bury your hands deep
inside the walls of my chest without flinching as
you grabbed my heart and held it in your hands
while I stared at the beautiful sight
Such a beautiful sight of you having my heart that
didn't lose its beauty until I realized that your face
didn't reciprocate my amazement but instead was
painted with malevolence, but I did nothing to
stop you I just gave you the benefit of the doubt
by thinking you were better
I just gave you the benefit of the doubt by thinking
you were better than having intentions of hurting
the thing that kept me alive, but I should have
looked through the light and seen the darkness
and realized your intentions were tragic

I should have looked through the light and seen the darkness and realized your intentions were tragic, but I couldn't because you were even more hurt than me

UNLESS I AM...

"Did you ever think that maybe living and being alive are two different things?" I asked her as she continued to scratch things down on her notepad. I wondered what she could possibly be writing about. No one could think so much about someone to be writing for 10 minutes straight. Unless she was writing, She's bat shit crazy, on a loop. Probably. I'm not crazy, despite everyone else's opinions. I just feel things. I feel things more than the normal person feels things. And we live in a world of labels, where if you feel things too much, you're depressed or crazy. Maybe even both. I think it's bullshit. Who established the line between feeling too much and feeling just the right amount, anyways? And who gave them the authority to establish that? Whoever that was must not have given a shit about anything.
"What do you mean," She asked as she continued writing, "Living and being alive are entirely the same. If you are living, you're alive and if you are alive, you're living." She recited as if she were reading the words she just spoke from a script.
"Then how can you feel so alive sometimes, and other times you feel so dead inside?"

"I-"

"Like, sometimes I feel awesome. I feel so great and I can accomplish anything. I feel alive. But sometimes I feel empty. And that's when I'm only living. I don't feel alive during that time, I only feel like I'm living," She finally looked up from her notepad and stared at me as I continued, "And people can make me feel alive or living, too. Some people make my bones feel alive. When I'm with them a rush flows through my body and I feel so fucking alive. More alive than ever. Other people don't have that effect on me, I'm with them and I don't feel that jitter in my bones or that smile inside of me. I just feel living. So, how can you tell me that living and being alive are the same thing?"

WAS IT MUDER IF I WISHED FOR IT?

He could palm a basketball, his hands were huge, and that's all I could think about when he used them against me. He made a fist and threw it into my face with every ounce of power his body contained.

I wondered where he learned to hit the way he did, so carelessly, like I had no feelings at all. He didn't give a fuck about them.

I remember the blood running down my face and mixing with my tears as I begged him to stop, to just leave me alone. I apologized repeatedly as he grabbed my head and slammed it into the wall. I felt pieces of dry wall on my face, sticking to the open wounds his fists made in my skin.

I'd like to think it was then that he realized he was going to kill me if he didn't stop. I'd like to think that he didn't think he was going to kill me, because he kept going. I don't remember what he hit me with next, but it was enough to knock me unconscious. Who knows what he did while I was unconscious?

I wish he would have killed me.

D _ P R _ S S _ _ N – AND NO, I DON'T WANT TO BUY ANY DAMN VOWELS

Laying in your bed at 12 AM trying to convince yourself that you can defeat the dark thoughts that are taking over your mind.

Getting out of bed at 1:30 AM and staring at your empty reflection in the mirror thinking about how pathetic you look.

Sobbing so loud at 2 you wake up your brother who comes in your room and says he wishes it would stop, having such little strength you do nothing but look at him and say, "I do too."

Holding a razor blade to your wrist that has the words "I AM ENOUGH" written across it at 2:30 and trying to think of just one reason not to push it into your skin.

Screaming into your tear-soaked pillow at 3 AM trying to feel something, trying to find a reason to stay.

DOES THE CALM COME FIRST OR LAST?

I am dark clouds
hiding the sunshine from the people in my world,
but only to make them appreciate it a little more.
Only to keep their worlds from burning to hell...
like mine did

I am rain
making the sky cry and infecting those around me
by creating a gloomy day, but only to keep my
roots alive. Only to give myself the water I need to
live... like you couldn't

I am wind
invisibly guiding things to places they don't know
they need to go and sometimes creating disaster,
but only to keep things fresh. Only to help myself
expand my horizons and explore... like I couldn't
with you

I am hail
expressing my anger and sadness through pieces
of the sky falling, not meaning to hurt others, but
only to release what I have bottled up. Only to
free my feelings... like you didn't want

I am thunder
causing loud, interrupting disturbances in lives of
those who are oblivious, but only to make my pain
known. Only to show them that someone out
there is hurting and needs them... like you never
saw

I am lightning
illuminating the sky with my pain and heartache,
but only to let it be seen. Only to let people know
that they are not alone... like you made me feel

I am a storm
never understood or appreciated and seen as a
burden, but only because I need to express myself.
Only because I need to feel okay... like you didn't
allow

And you?

You are the calm
feeling only content and happiness within yourself
and your life, but only after you've ripped a world
apart. Only after you've destroyed things... like me

THE GIRL YOU KILLED.

Get up I said in my head as I evaluated the
situation I was in
"Get up" I said out loud to myself as I stood up
and dusted myself off
I dusted myself off and as the dirt left, he did too
He left too, just like everyone else

"Marlboro blacks" I asked of the cashier who in
return asked for my ID
"Thank you" I blurted out instinctively as she
handed me the pack
The cigarettes that he thought would kill me
The cigarettes I promised him I'd never smoke
again
Smoking again was all I wanted to do
All I wanted to do was light fire to my insides

Fuck I thought as I inhaled a puff and coughed
"Fuck" I said out loud at the feeling it produced in
my body
My body needed to feel the lightness from the
cigarettes
Cigarettes became my safe place
My safe place used to be you, but you killed me

You killed me more than the cigarettes ever did

WHO THE HELL SAYS THAT TIME HEALS?

It's been one year
And I still walk with my head up looking for your
face in the crowd of strangers on the sidewalk
every day hoping that today you'll show up
because I swear, I finally have the courage to talk
to you

It's been fifty-two weeks
And I still go to bed every night praying to a god I
don't know if I believe in that he'll somehow free
me from my nightmares of you tonight because I
keep reliving the morning you left me

It's been three hundred sixty-five days
And I still wake up in the morning without the
knowledge of your absence in my life and because
of it I must remind myself with my phone alarm
that rings "he's gone, you're okay" and 9 AM

It's been eight thousand seven hundred sixty hours
And I still flinch when I hear your name like a thousand knives are being thrown my way and I can't manage to dodge them all because there's too many, so I just let them cut me because pain means nothing anymore

It's been five hundred twenty-five thousand six hundred minutes
And I still do a double take when I see a black car like yours and remember all the times we sang in the front seat but remind myself that those times are over and won't come again

It's been thirty-one million five hundred thirty-six thousand seconds
And I still hope you text me to check up and ask how I am so I can tell you I still love you, but I guess you know better than I do that some things are better left unsaid

It's been one year
And I miss you

BLACKOUT POETRY.

She felt pain abruptly because his smile was her
signal of strength and he left.

YOU LOVED ME BECAUSE YOU THOUGHT
YOU SHOULD.

Don't come back and tell me you miss me and you
only left because you loved me more than you
knew what to do with because you never told me
how much you loved me while you were here and
now I don't know what to believe

WHAT IF I WAS ALWAYS MEANT TO –

Give up.

AA.

He was my addiction and I was the raving addict who couldn't live without him.

ACKNOWLEDGMENTS.

First, thank you for reading.
Second, thank *you* for giving me something to write about.

INSIGHT.

I believe that we live in a world where people are afraid to express and be open about their dark, yet genuine feelings. Maybe that's why I've always felt like I don't belong here, or maybe I just see things different.

Expressing these feelings is forever and always OKAY and should be more widely accepted. Especially among young individuals. Having feelings or experiences that are like the ones in this book, or even entirely different, isn't something to fret over. It doesn't make you a bad person. It doesn't make you a miserable person. It doesn't make you someone who isn't enjoyable to be around. It doesn't make you impossible. It doesn't make you unworthy. It doesn't make you worthless. It doesn't make you less of a person. It doesn't make you annoying. It doesn't make you attention seeking. It makes you one beautiful fucking human.

Read that paragraph again. And again.

If this book gives you anything, let it be openness. It could save your damn life. I know it saved mine.

Made in the USA
Lexington, KY
13 February 2019